HOW TO AVOID
THE
CUTTING ROOM FLOOR

AN EDITOR'S ADVICE
FOR ON-CAMERA ACTORS

JORDAN GOLDMAN, A.C.E.

How to Avoid the Cutting Room Floor:
An editor's advice for on-camera actors

1.3 Edition

Copyright © 2014 Jordan Goldman. All rights reserved.

Print Edition

Back cover portrait by Prashant Gupta (prashant-gupta.com)

TABLE OF CONTENTS

INTRODUCTION

The most terrifying day of my life was the day I "acted" on camera.

We were shooting the final episode of *The Shield*. Word came up to the cutting rooms that the director, Clark Johnson, wanted me on set to do a cameo. I was told I'd be a janitor crossing in the background of the police station.

I walked over to the set, where Wardrobe gave me a set of coveralls and work boots. Then I was handed a mop. The Assistant Director said, "During the scene, you're going to exit the bathroom and walk across the bullpen to the motor pool hallway."

As the crew scurried around setting up the shot, I stood alone in the bathroom and started to worry about what I was supposed to do. It had been a long time since I'd been in musicals back in high school. Was I really up to this? My mind flooded with questions. What was my motivation to go to the motor pool hallway? Was I heading to a spill? Then I should be in in a hurry. Or had I already finished cleaning up the problem? Then I should act more relaxed. But why was my mop dry? If I was leaving the bathroom then the mop should be wet, because I had either used it to clean a spill, or just dampened it to clean something. Wouldn't it make more sense if I had been filling a bucket here in the bathroom and was taking my mop and bucket to the site of the spill? But it was too late to convince Props to give me a bucket — we were about to roll!

The ADs locked down the set. I realized that I didn't know what my cue was to come out of the bathroom. Everyone assumed that because I worked on the show, I'd know what to do. But I had no idea. Should I exit on action? Halfway through the scene? What was I supposed to do? There was nobody in the bathroom to ask. A small panic attack started to brew. It seemed clear to me that if I screwed up this cross, it would ruin the entire scene. On TV, the police station would seem like it was full of real people (the actual actors) and one dummy pretending to be a janitor. I was on the verge of ruining everything and letting down all of my friends. On the final episode of the entire series, no less!

I heard "action!" With no idea of what else to do, I waited for a five count, then stepped out of the bathroom carrying my mop. Before my very eyes, the 40-foot long bullpen set seemed to telescope out into a room four miles long. The motor pool hallway was almost visible far in the distance like a pot of gold at the end of a rainbow. Somehow I managed to will myself into motion. When I finally got to the motor pool hallway a thousand terrifying years later, I passed the room where Clark and the rest of the crew were watching the take on the video monitors. Through the door I could clearly hear Clark exclaim, "What the hell is with that janitor? Why is he running across the room like that?"

I thought I would die. After the AD called cut, I slowly crawled back to the bathroom. I was too embarrassed to look at anyone. (In retrospect, I'm pretty sure Clark said that as loudly as he could just to mess with me. Along with being a great director and generous mentor, he's a notorious prankster.)

My friend Rich Cantu, the B-camera operator, must have seen the terror in my eyes. He pulled me aside and spoke to me in clear, short words. "When you hear Dutch's second line, come out of the bathroom. Walk to the motor pool hallway. Maybe a little slower this time."

Thanks to Rich, things got better in subsequent takes, and if you watch episode 713 of *The Shield*, I'm in there, somehow managing to cross the room without looking completely fake. Luckily, I was able to make sure that the ridiculous janitor didn't ruin the scene... because I was also the editor of that episode.

But what if I had gone through all of that terror and then been cut out of the show? What if I was a real actor, who had prepared and auditioned and worked hard for this moment, and I was cut out? I would have been very upset. I imagine every one of you reading this book would be really disappointed if you watched a project you'd acted in, only to realize that you had been cut out. Well, now you have a secret weapon — this book. You can walk into the situation far better prepared than most actors. I'm going to help you avoid winding up on the cutting room floor.

There's a lot of things you can do to prevent yourself from being cut out, most of which you can rehearse before you ever arrive on the set. But there are also some things you can't control. We'll cover both.

You can use the principles in this book to boost your on-camera work whether you're acting in a student film, a TV show, or a blockbuster feature film. I talk a lot about television in this book, and mostly about drama shows, but the principles apply to all genres of on-camera acting.

If you do a good job of believably representing the character you've been hired to portray, avoid alienating people on set, and are able to perform the technical necessities like remembering your lines and hitting your marks, then you've done everything you can. That's what you can control. What happens next is out of your control. Some of your lines, or even your entire performance, might still be cut from the show through no fault of your own. Your material might be cut to prevent the show from being too long, or because your scene (or character, or lines) slowed down the momentum of the story. This is the core of my message, but I'm going to give you much greater detail in the chapters that follow.

If you can't master your technical skills or produce a good performance, then there's not much we can do in Editorial to save you. Believe it or not, editors get no pleasure from cutting hard-working actors out of the show, especially those actors who don't have many lines. We want to showcase actors and honor their hard work.

But we do get pleasure from cutting out bad performances, because they are dragging down the quality of our project. The editor's ultimate job is to serve the story, and if what the actor is doing isn't supporting the story, then we have to work around them.

I don't want to cut you out. I want you to shine. I love actors and the amazing work that you do. I know just how lucky I am to see so much of your wonderful work up close. Let me tell you what I've learned in the cutting room, so we can help each other to make something great.

CHAPTER 1

IT'S ALL ABOUT THE SETUPS

Everything that precedes editing is merely a way of
producing film to edit.

— Stanley Kubrick

The crew and actors go to the set and they film a scene. They don't film the scene once and then go home. They shoot it many, many times from several different angles. Each angle is called a "setup."

Why so many setups, and so many takes?

Playing an entire scene in one size can be visually monotonous. The director avoids this problem by filming the same action from several different angles.

She keeps filming takes until she feels she's captured the ideal performance from each actor. The director may experiment with the actors from take to take, changing the rhythm and emotional intensity of the scene, so she winds up with different interpretations of the scene that she can combine in the cutting room. She's also shooting until her camera moves and focus racks are correctly performed by the camera and grip crews.

By providing us with many different angles, the director gives us flexibility in the editing room. We can assemble the scene in any shot order we want. We can choose how we want to play any given moment. A character's big entrance doesn't have to be in a close-up. Depending on the needs of the scene, it might be better in a wide shot, or in a Stedicam follow shot, or in an interesting racking shot. A good director will shoot several options, so we can make the best choice in Editorial. Sometimes the best choice doesn't become evident until long after filming, so the more choices we have, the better.

An editor can improve performances or emphasize the drama of a moment by deciding when to cut from one angle to another. This is the bread and butter of our craft. Each actor in a conversation between two characters will be filmed several times, in progressively closer sizes. As the scene unfolds, the editor will move the audience closer to the characters by cutting from the wider takes to the closer takes. The size change subtly tells viewers that something important is happening in the scene, and it increases the audience's connection to the characters. We couldn't do this if the whole scene was filmed in one size.

Having multiple setups allows us to solve problems. If we can't stay in a certain take of a close-up because the actor forgot their line halfway through, having additional angles enable us to cut to a different camera position and take to keep the actor's performance moving. Problem solved. But in order to make these kinds of saves, we need lots of different setups!

Let's say we're shooting a film called *Blackmailed Beauty*. In the climactic scene, our protagonist Elaine meets her tormentor Joe at a diner. Twenty years ago in high school, they used to run in the same crowd. But now Joe is blackmailing Elaine. Elaine has brought a gun to their meeting. It's in her purse, and she's considering shooting Joe right here in the diner to put an end to her problems. Here's the script of this 2 ⅛-page scene, which I'll be using throughout the book to illustrate concepts.

BLACKMAILED BEAUTY

EXT. DINER - DAY

Outside a Los Angeles diner.

INT. DINER - DAY

The diner is virtually empty. ELAINE enters.
Not interested in the ambience. Dreading what
awaits her.

She looks around, sees the person she's
looking for - JOE. She makes a beeline for the
table where he sits waiting for her.

She stands a beat, staring at him, then sits.
She keeps her purse on her lap. There are two
coffee mugs on the table.

                    JOE
          You're late, Elaine.

                    ELAINE
          I'm here, OK?

A WAITRESS steps forward with a menu for
Elaine.

                    WAITRESS
               (to Joe)
          This must be your friend.

She puts the menu in front of Elaine. Elaine
doesn't look at it.

                    WAITRESS
          Let me know when you're ready.

She moves off.

                                   (CONTINUED)

The pair sit in silence for a moment.

                    JOE
          I ordered you a coffee.
            (gestures at the mug)
          You still two sugars, no milk?
            (off her)
          Have some. You seem tense.

Elaine thinks it over, then mechanically picks
up the mug, drinks some, puts it down.

                    JOE
          You bring the money?

                    ELAINE
          Why are you doing this to me,
          Joe?

                    JOE
          You did this to yourself. You
          don't get to be Mrs. Governor and
          pretend you were never one of us.

                    ELAINE
          My life doesn't have anything to
          do with you anymore. Why won't
          you let go?

                    JOE
          'Cause you can afford it. Now
          where's the money?

                    ELAINE
          How do I know you're going to
          stop if I pay you?

                    JOE
          My good word.

                              (CONTINUED)

She gives him a look. She knows him too well
for that.

                    ELAINE
          So there's no guarantee.

Joe is silent. Under the table, Elaine slips a
hand into the purse on her lap.

                    ELAINE
          Just say it. I want to hear you
          say it.

                    JOE
          You taping this?

                    ELAINE
          You know I'm not.

                    JOE
          Ok. There is no guarantee. I own
          you.

Elaine pulls a handgun from her purse.
She stands and points the gun at Joe's face.
He is so surprised that he doesn't even dodge
the muzzle.

                    ELAINE
          You bastard, you've ruined my
          life. You pushed and pushed and
          now I don't have a choice.

Elaine pulls the trigger and shoots Joe in the
face. He falls back like a sack of potatos.

Patrons SCREAM.

Elaine turns and runs from the diner, acting
like she's one of the frightened crowd.

To tell the story of a scene, the director will shoot "coverage" — the various angles and shots which cover the action. They'll usually begin by shooting a traditional "master shot" and then move in closer to cover specific characters or moments.

Without coverage, the editor has no choices within the scene. We are forced to play the whole scene in a continuous take of the wide shot, from start to end, with no ability to emphasize moments, improve performances, or avoid problems by cutting to other angles.

For the *Blackmailed Beauty* scene, the director will probably shoot the following coverage of fifteen shots:

(1) an establishing shot, which shows the outside of the diner

(2) the master shot — an interior wide shot showing the general setting, including the location of Elaine and Joe's table

(3) a medium-wide shot — similar to the wide, but closer

(4) a shot that pans across the table between Joe and Elaine

Dedicated coverage of Joe — note how the camera moves closer and closer:

(5) an over-the-shoulder

(6) an over-the-shoulder medium

(7) a clean medium close-up

(8) a clean close-up

Dedicated coverage of Elaine:

(9) an over-the-shoulder

(10) an over-the-shoulder medium

(11) a clean medium close-up

(12) a clean close-up

(13) a close-up of Elaine's hand
reaching into her purse for the gun

(14) a shot over Elaine standing, looking down at Joe

(15) a shot over Joe, looking up at Elaine
pointing the gun at him

Usually four or five takes of each setup will be filmed. Once the director is satisfied with the camerawork and the actors' performances in each setup, the crew "moves on" to the next setup.

Because shooting time is very valuable on a TV set (one-hour dramas typically have only 8 days to film an episode), there will usually be two cameras rolling on every take. This enables the crew to film two angles simultaneously (such as Joe's clean medium and his clean close-up), allowing more work to be accomplished in a day.

After each take, the director confers privately with the script supervisor. If the director liked the take, he tells the script super to "print it." This expression is a throwback to the film days, where you'd save money by not developing, or "printing," every take. Nowadays, "Print that" has become shorthand for "I like that take."

**WHAT IS
A SCRIPT SUPERVISOR?**

The script supervisor (also referred to as the "Script Super" or "Scripty") sits next to the director at the video monitors.

Scripty serves many functions on set, but for our purposes, their most important task is to watch during filming to make sure that everything is the same from take to take. They follow along with the script to make sure that the correct words are spoken (if you yell "Line!" it's Scripty who answers back), they double-check that the wardrobe and props are consistent from scene to scene (so a character doesn't exit one scene holding a pistol and enter the next holding a rifle), and that the actors perform the same actions at exactly the same time in each take (such as when you remove your sunglasses).

At the end of the day, Scripty sends paperwork to the editing room that tells us what has been filmed, from what angles, and what the director's opinion of each take was.

The director will usually print at least two takes of each setup. He may give the script supervisor some notes to pass on to the editor, such as "Take 4 is only good for the opening of the scene" or "Take 3 is good for Joe, but not good for Elaine."

At the conclusion of shooting, the crew will have filmed far more footage than will appear in the final product. It's not uncommon to shoot forty minutes worth of dailies for a scene that will only be two minutes long on screen.

CHAPTER 2

WHAT DOES AN EDITOR DO?

Every block of stone has a statue inside it,
and it is the task of the sculptor to discover it.

— *Michelangelo*

Now that the crew has shot all of the angles and takes, it's up to the editor to choose the best pieces and seamlessly put them together into a compelling scene.

I begin by watching everything that was filmed for the scene. Then I select the ideal setup for each moment of the scene, and decide which take of that angle to use, based on the quality of the actors' performances and the camera work. I work my way through the scene moment by moment, building my "cut" out of all the best pieces.

A large part of my job is evaluating the actors' performances, then elevating them as best I can. That means being realistic about who is working well in the scenes, and who isn't. I've edited all kinds of actors — awful ones, amazing award-winning ones, and actors who performed terribly on set but looked brilliant once they were pieced together from many different takes. My job is to make them all look great.

Most people assume that I start cutting with the director sitting alongside me, telling me what takes and angles to use, but that's not so. The director can't be in Editorial with me until they've finished the whole shoot.

So I start cutting by myself while the director continues filming.

I rely on the script supervisor's paperwork and the dailies to tell me what the director is thinking. They will point me towards the performances the director was aiming for. I won't see the director until two or three days after shooting has finished, by which time I will have done a cut of the entire show on my own. So the editor (with some guidance from Scripty's notes) is the person who makes the initial decision about which performances appear on screen.

Because I'm not on the set, I have a different perspective than the director. My perspective is unclouded by the struggle to capture the footage. I only see the footage as it exists, without any backstory from the set. Whether a shot was difficult or easy to film makes no difference to my analysis of its worth. Being removed from the set gives me a clarity that people directly involved in the day-to-day shooting may not be able to obtain.

When I watch the dailies, sometimes I don't agree with the director about which take is best. The director is surrounded by chaos and pressure on set. They have to make very quick decisions and can't easily compare what they just shot to what they shot ten minutes ago, or even ten days ago. But in the cutting room, it's just me in a dark room with a big TV. I have lots of time to watch takes over and over again, to compare moments, and to think deeply about the performances, the story, and what the actors are doing. I think about what each character has already been through, and what's going to happen to them later in the story. I think about their beat-by-beat objectives. I think about their arc within the scene and within the larger show. I think about the tone meeting we had before the episode began shooting, where the showrunner talked about their goals for each scene and for the larger episode. All of these factors are in play when I am judging performances. Then I start making decisions about how to construct the scene and which takes to use.

> ### WHAT IS A SHOWRUNNER?
>
> The showrunner is the top executive producer, the person who guides the overall creative direction of the show. They are usually the creator of the show and also the head writer.
>
> Examples – Aaron Sorkin on *The West Wing*, Alex Gansa on *Homeland*, Kurt Sutter on *Sons Of Anarchy*, Vince Gilligan on *Breaking Bad*, Shonda Rhimes on *Grey's Anatomy*, Chuck Lorre on *Big Bang Theory*.
>
> In the film world, the director is King, but in television the showrunner is King. The showrunner usually has the last word on how the show is edited.

In the course of assembling the scene, I'll decide which angle to use for each moment, which size (closer or tighter), and which take of that size to use.

At the beginning of each scene, I'll generally want to show the audience the space where the action is taking place and who is in the room, so I'll probably start with a wide shot. If I want to withhold information from the audience about where we are, or who is in the room, then I can start in closer coverage and wait until just the right moment to use the wide shot to reveal things. For example,

I could start close on Elaine talking to Joe on the phone, then cut wide to reveal she's surrounded by detectives listening in. Because the editor controls what the audience sees, the editor can also control what the audience knows and feels.

As the scene progresses and the conflict heats up, we'll generally move from wider shots to closer shots, thus allowing the audience to get closer and closer to the actors' faces and see their emotions more clearly.

Throughout the process, I'll do whatever I can to bolster all of the actors' performances. My personal opinion is that performance is the most important thing in a scene, so I will always choose an average shot of a great performance over a beautiful shot of a bland performance. Sometimes I will even use a take which has slight camera focus problems if the performance is really incredible. (What am I looking for in a performance? That's Chapter 5.)

Most viewers don't realize that editors often take pieces from different takes to build the actor's final performance. Let's assume the director filmed five takes of Elaine's close-up. That means I can mine five different close-up performances for the beats I need. Generally I will see one performance that stands out above the others, and that becomes my go-to take. I'll try to use that take whenever I cut to Elaine's close-up. Let's say her best performance was the last one, take 5.

But there may be some lines or moments that Elaine didn't quite nail in take 5. She did an interesting look that

I liked in take 4 after Joe said, "My good word." In take 3, when she said "My life doesn't have anything to do with you anymore," she put an extra slap on the reading that I really liked. The camera badly missed focus when Elaine leaned forward to get the coffee mug in take 5, so I need a different take for that action.

The audience shouldn't realize I'm switching takes, so if everyone did their job correctly on set, Elaine will appear to be sitting in the exact same place in every take, with the exact same lighting and the exact same background action happening around her. I also need to be careful that switching takes doesn't upset her emotional through-line, so I can't cut from a take where she is elated to a take where she has tears of sorrow running down her face. She needs to be in the same emotional space from cut to cut, or transitioning from one emotional state to another, otherwise the audience will know I pulled a trick on them.

Every time I cut to Joe, I get to choose which take of Elaine to return to. Likewise, after I cut to Elaine, I get to choose which take of Joe to return to. I only have to stay in a take for as long as it's good. Once it starts to go south, I can cut to a different take or shot where the performance didn't falter (or where something more interesting started happening). In this way, I can edit the scene so the audience only sees the best on-camera performance from each actor for any given moment.

If I'm building my cut around take 5 of Elaine, but I want to get that look from take 4 in, here's how I'd do it.

I'd start with Elaine's take 5 for her line of dialogue before the look — "How do I know you're going to stop if I pay you?"

Then I'd cut to Joe for his line that triggers the look — "My good word."

When I cut back to Elaine for her look, I can use her take 4 and nobody will ever know I changed takes.

I'll cut back to Joe to see his response to her look...

...and when I return to Elaine's shot for "So there's no guarantee," I can be back in good old take 5.

Take 5

Shawn Ryan, the creator/showrunner of *The Shield*, used to say, "The actor only has to get the performance right once [in each setup]," meaning it's OK if an actor is mediocre in four takes of the close-up, as long as they nail it in the fifth take. Technically he's right, but I'm sure you want to be the kind of actor who nails it in every take and doesn't rely on the editor to save you. You can take heart in his message, because when I see your magic take, I'm going to try to use it every time I cut to you. I'm going to build my cutting pattern around that wonderful take. So if you go home feeling awful that you batted one-out-of-five, don't worry too much. I saw that fifth take. Once the show leaves my cutting room, nobody else will ever know about the first four. Just make sure to send me a fruit basket when you win your Emmy.

Sometimes there's a take where I like the camera-work or your facial expression, but your line reading wasn't as good as a read you did in another take. In this situation, I can try to replace the audio of the "bad" read with the audio of the "good" read to get the best of both worlds. It only works if the timing and rhythm of the performances is the same, otherwise your lips won't match what we're hearing. When someone wants me to do this in the cutting room, they'll ask, "Can you put the good take in his mouth?"

We often cheat reaction shots as well. A reaction shot is a silent shot of one character reacting to another character. Reaction shots help the audience track what the characters are thinking as the scene progresses. For instance, if the school principal is droning on endlessly, we'll want to cut to a shot of a bored, yawning teacher. That's a good reaction shot. Editors will pull reaction shots from any part of any take they can, as long as the shot conveys the right message. That piece of the teacher yawning might have come from after the director yelled "Cut!" (Good camera operators keep filming for a few seconds after cut is called, specifically so they can capture those kind of nuggets.)

It's very interesting to see the effect of someone's words on the person they are talking to. Imagine a husband telling a wife that he is leaving her. Who is more interesting to watch as he says the words? The husband having the courage to say it, or the wife reacting to the bad news? That's why we sometimes don't stay on an actor for the full run of their dialogue. Partway through, we cut to the listener so the audience can see what that character is thinking. This also gives us the opportunity to switch takes on the speaker when we cut back from the listener!

Often I will elongate or shorten the space between when one actor finishes their line and the other actor begins theirs. A long pause can create anxiety or make the character appear unsure of what they are going to say. A short pause has the opposite effect. It makes the character appear to be more certain and engaged. For example, when Joe asks, "Are you taping this?" imagine there is a long pause before Elaine replies, "You know I'm not." That pause would make her behavior seem suspicious. Maybe she is taping him and can't decide whether to lie about it. But if she answers instantly, she'll seem impatient and angry that he'd accuse her. In the cutting room, if someone wants me to make the actors respond to each other more quickly, they'll tell me to "pick up the cues" in the scene or "cut out the air."

Along with working the performances, I'll also add sound effects to the scene (such as the background sound of diner patrons, phone rings, gun shots, etc.) and music (like the ominous strings that play as Elaine decides whether to pull out the gun).

When I'm satisfied with my cut of the scene, I'll put it away and move on to the next scene, where my process starts all over again.

CHAPTER 3

THE PROCESS IN TELEVISION

No matter what accomplishments you make,
somebody helped you.

— *Althea Gibson*

After I've cut every scene, I'll assemble them all into one long sequence to "build" the full show. I'll look at the episode as a whole and make some changes, then I'll send my "Editor's Cut" to the director.

This will be the first time anyone else has seen the show, because Directors Guild rules mandate that my Editor's Cut is for the director's eyes only. That avoids a situation where the director is judged for my mistakes if I do a bad job. Imagine if I have chosen all the worst takes and ugliest angles for a scene and, before the director has a chance to see and fix it, the showrunner comes to my room and says, "Hey, show me that scene!" I show her my awful cut. The showrunner thinks to herself, "I'd better fire this director right now, before he ruins the rest of the episode." It would be an unfair judgment because good takes and footage exist. I just didn't put them in. The director deserves the opportunity to present a cut to the showrunner that accurately reflects what he was trying to accomplish on set.

After receiving the Editor's Cut, the director has four working days with me to make whatever changes they desire. Along with doing things like changing the cutting pattern of a scene and adjusting music, they will experiment with different performances. I may have selected a take where Joe tries to charm Elaine, but the director wants to use the one where Joe bullies her instead. So we swap it out. When we are done with all of the changes, we send the "Director's Cut" to the show's executive producers and showrunner.

Next, the showrunner will work with me for a week or so to make any changes they want. This is usually when lines of dialogue and parts of scenes will be eliminated in the interest of getting the show down to the required length and making the story better. Performances will be tweaked to make emotional through-lines clearer and more consistent. The order of scenes may be re-arranged. New lines of dialogue may be added to make plot points clearer. In extreme cases, we may realize that new scenes are needed as well.

STUDIOS AND NETWORKS

Many television networks produce shows which air on other networks. For example, a subsidiary of Fox called "Fox21" produces *Homeland* and licenses it to Showtime for broadcast in the United States. The American public considers *Homeland* to be a Showtime show, but in reality, Fox is the studio and Showtime is the network.

We send the "Producer's Cut" to the studio, which is the company that initially develops and finances the show. They give us a round of notes. The showrunner and I confer on which of the notes to implement. The result of these changes becomes the "Studio Cut," which is then sent to the network that broadcasts the show.

The network may request a round or two of changes, producing iterations of the "Network Cut." After the last set of notes have been given, the showrunner returns to my cutting room and we do some final tweaks. When we are done, the cut is considered "locked," which means no further changes will be made to the picture. My assistant editor hands the show over to the colorist, the composer, visual effects department, sound editors, and mixers so they can do their magic. It's time for me to move on to my next episode.

It takes about a month for an episode of a one-hour drama to get through the editing process. During that time, the crew will have shot two more episodes. One editor can't keep up with the workload. So one-hour dramas generally have three editors on staff working in a fixed rotation. I cut episode 1, the second editor cuts episode 2, the third editor cuts episode 3, and by then I'm finished with episode 1 and available again to cut episode 4. We follow this pattern for the whole season.

Many different parties have an opportunity to give their opinions on the episode during the editorial process, but only one person is there for all of it — me. Through all of these sets of notes and revisions, I hear what the decision makers say about the actors and their perform-ances. And the decision makers listen to my input as well. So let's pull back the curtain and let you in on it, too.

CHAPTER 4

WHAT DO DIRECTORS, PRODUCERS, WRITERS, SHOWRUNNERS, EXECUTIVES, AND EDITORS REALLY THINK OF ACTORS?

Just say the lines and don't bump into the furniture.

— *Noel Coward*

For the most part, we love actors! Sure, some of them are a pain in the ass, a few are much more trouble than they're worth, but the vast majority are good people working hard to help bring our story to life. What matters most to us is whether the actor can deliver.

The primary tasks of the actor, as awful as this may sound, are to:

- stand in the right places

- say the right words

- be directable

- convince the audience that you are the person the story claims you to be...

- ...experiencing the events and emotions that the story claims you are experiencing.

If you can't accomplish those basic goals, then you're not doing what you were hired for, and you become a problem that needs to be edited around.

If you can do those five things, then you're doing exactly what's expected of you. You are fulfilling your part in the storytelling machine and you're not sticking out as something that doesn't fit with everything else on screen. Good job!

If you bring something fresh, interesting, or original to the role, then you move yourself up a rank to someone who's **adding** to the story. Not just doing the minimum needed, but actually elevating the material. I'm talking about things like bringing an interesting point-of-view on a scene, or an interesting interpretation of who your character is (more on point-of-view later). Directors remember those actors. So do writers, editors, and producers. They also remember the actors who can't do the basics, and make sure not to hire them again. An interesting point-of-view from someone who can't hit their marks doesn't do us much good. You need to be able to do the basics. After that you can fly.

When someone is unable to do the basics, then we all start to dislike them. I'm sorry if that sounds harsh, but it is true. Over the course of editing a single episode, I'll probably watch every scene a hundred times. Every time I watch a well-written moment fail because of a bad actor, I curse that actor in my head. So do the bosses sitting behind me, like the showrunner and the director. Every time a scene goes by and I remember that we had to remove a wonderful moment because the actor couldn't land it, I resent that actor again. I can't help it. That moment/line/look was so good on the page, why couldn't they just do it convincingly? I know acting is a tough job, but if that's the job you signed up for and are being paid to do, then you should do it right.

You need to remember that your desire for artistic self-expression is **secondary** to your obligation to be a vessel for the showrunner's vision. They hired to you to play a part a certain way. Your character plays a function in this scene, in this episode, in this series. You're a cog in a bigger machine. If you do your job poorly, then the showrunner has to work around the loss of that cog and make other plans. When a bad actor does a bad job in a critical part… well, that character needs to be retired and a new one written who will accomplish the same dramatic function in future episodes. Maybe the showrunner will kill that character, or the character gets fired, or the character is re-assigned to another office. Maybe the character simply never shows up again, with no explanation given. I've seen it a few times. The showrunner says, "We had plans for that character, but the actor's just terrible. He's never going to be able to do what we planned. Now I gotta figure out something else." I know it's disappointing for the actor — but honestly it's a relief to me, because now I know the story can go forward properly, performed by someone who will do the job well.

A bad attitude can earn the actor the same fate. In Mandatory.com's *An Oral History of The Shield* (mandatory.com/2013/09/10/good-cop-bad-cop-an-oral-history-of-the-shield), Shawn Ryan said, "A lot of the time, when a character has a surprising death on a TV show, you can bet pretty good money that that actor was a pain in the ass in some way." (For all you *Shield* fans out there — this was certainly not the case with our show, it's more of a reflection on the industry in general.)

If you do your job well, the powers-that-be will notice and praise you. And if the right opportunity arises, they are likely to hire you again. Early in the first season of *Homeland*, our show's co-creators were having difficulty finding the right actor to play Danny Galvez, a recurring member of the CIA team. Finally Howard Gordon said, "Why don't we get Hrach Titizian? He did a good job for us on *24* and he'd do well here." Everyone agreed, and that was it. Good work and a good attitude had kept Hrach in the producers' minds, and eventually won him another role.

The writer wants someone who can bring their words to life.

The director wants someone who is convincing, can take direction, and get the job done in time. An actor who brings something to the table that adds to what the director is trying to do is a bonus.

The showrunner wants someone who is close to or better than what they had in their head when they read or wrote the script. They want someone who fulfills the function of the character, and doesn't need to be removed in order for the story to work.

And me? I want all of the same things they do. But most of all, I want someone who feels real. In my eyes, the biggest sin you can commit, the one thing I can't help you overcome through my editing, is for you to be unconvincing.

(There's a bunch of other things I want too. They make up the rest of this book. But an actor who is not convincing really is my most insurmountable problem.)

CHAPTER 5

WHAT YOU CAN CONTROL:
YOUR PERFORMANCE

Acting is behaving truthfully under imaginary circumstances.

— *Sanford Meisner*

When we're watching your footage in the cutting room, we're looking for the same performance techniques your acting teacher drilled into you time after time. Here's where their lessons pay off. If you follow these principles, you are much more likely to end up on screen. They are all things that you have complete control over, if you use your instrument properly.

Be believable. For the illusion of our story to hold, everyone needs to do their part. The cinematographer and production designer make the world look real. The sound team makes it sound real. The actors must make the people inhabiting it seem real. As soon as something fake appears in the frame, the audience gets distracted and the whole house of cards comes tumbling down. That's why your believability is so crucial.

So think to yourself — who is your character? Inhabit that person and behave accordingly.

If you're playing a cop, you can't have a timid, anxious approach like you would if you were a mousy librarian. Cops take ownership of the spaces they move through; that's part of what makes them intimidating.

So if you're a cop — be a cop.

When I see someone who feels real, I want to give them screen time because they're contributing to the believability of our fictional world. If they're interesting, I want to watch them. One day when I was working on *The Shield*, another editor called me into his room to watch an amazing take of someone playing a prison guard. In the scene, the actor strode up a crowded prison hallway giving orders to the prisoners. When I watched him, I felt like I was in prison. It was incredible. The actor was so alpha he scared the crap out of me. Guess what? That editor worked hard to put in as much of that actor's performance as he could.

The reverse situation? I've had any number of actors cross my screen playing cops who seemed more like accountants with guns. When the front door is opened for the accounta-cops, they look right at the homeowner instead of scanning the room for potential threats. The accounta-cops wait politely for the people they're questioning to respond. Instead of grabbing the suspect's hands for cuffing, they wait for the suspect to move their own hands into the right position. I cut those inauthentic actors' screen time to the minimum possible, as fast as I can. Hopefully I can eliminate them altogether, because they are ruining the illusion of our show.

Please... don't be an accounta-cop.

We don't want to watch someone pretending to be a cop — we want to watch someone who we think actually is a cop! Your job as an actor is to convince us that you are really that person. Don't be an actor who is pretending to be that person. The better you are at inhabiting everything about the character, the more we want you on screen so we can watch you.

Be honest. A great actor/director I've worked with once said about another actor's performance, "He's playing the idea of being upset, instead of actually being upset." What a great critique! We want to watch someone who is connected to the material and connected to their own emotions. That produces a performance which feels real, instead of an actor reciting lines. It's moving to watch, which makes me try to highlight it however I can.

Show a point-of-view. This is something that Kurt Sutter, the showrunner of *Sons Of Anarchy,* would often say. Don't be a body in some clothes standing mindlessly as the life of the scene goes on around you. Your character has an opinion and an attitude about every person they encounter. Maybe your character hates the other person, maybe they love the other person, maybe they are annoyed by the other person, maybe they're trying to ignore the other person. Those are all distinct points-of-view that can be played. Over the course of the scene, your attitude about the other characters will likely change. That's interesting to watch too.

Having a strong point-of-view will naturally create interesting behavior. As an actor, knowing your character's attitude about the people surrounding you and the situation you are in will help you figure out how to play the scene.

In *Blackmailed Beauty*, when Elaine walks into the diner, she's focused on dealing with blackmailer Joe, a man who is hurting her. She hates him. That's her point-of-view, and all of her other choices will fall into place accordingly. One look at Elaine's face when she sits down across from Joe should tell us exactly how she feels about him.

Elaine's point-of-view towards the diner's staff and customers is different than her point-of-view towards Joe. She doesn't hate the waitress passionately. She probably doesn't even register the waitress' existence because she's so lasered in on Joe. If the waitress tried to take food orders and Elaine was forced to interact with her, Elaine should want to end the conversation as fast as possible.

Elaine should have a point-of-view about everything that is said or done in the scene. When blackmailer Joe says, "You did this to yourself. You don't get to be Mrs. Governor and pretend you were never one of us," how does Elaine feel about being accused of betraying her old friends? Does she ignore it and keep quiet, or is there a flash of anger? Whichever reaction the actress chooses to convey, I want to see it.

Remember in *Silence of the Lambs* when Jodie Foster's character Clarice goes to the prison to meet Hannibal Lecter for the first time? First she's warned by the arrogant Warden about how Lecter mauled a nurse who wasn't paying attention, and then she's shown a graphic photo of what's left of the nurse's face. They send her down a long medieval prison hallway, where she has to pass several cells and their crazy inhabitants on her way to Lecter. Jodie Foster's face shows us exactly how Clarice feels about the environment she's in and the monster she is about to meet. Her point-of-view is crystal clear!

How would a bad actor with no point-of-view have handled the same scene?

By acting as if the terrible things the Warden was warning her about weren't terrible. By walking down the prison hall the same way she'd walk through a shopping mall. By reacting the same way to meeting Lecter as she would to meeting her mailman for the first time.

You may argue that the bad actress is making valid character choices. I say that there is a big difference between having no point-of-view and **trying to hide** your point-of-view from the characters around you. The bad actor has no point-of-view. She's not putting on a brave face — she's just using her regular face. If you watch *Silence of the Lambs*, you'll notice that Jodie Foster is actually trying to keep her fear to herself and not let any of the other characters know how she feels. That's a character choice, one which helps cement the audience's connection with Clarice.

Here's an example of an unrealistic point-of-view, which has clearly been dictated by a writer or director before the actor ever got to set: many times on *Law & Order*, the detectives would go to a workplace and question someone. The character they're questioning often keeps going about their work during the Q&A. They're putting folders on desks, stocking shelves and so forth, as if they get questioned by the cops every day and it's no big thing. That kind of blasé behavior makes sense for a career criminal who is often in trouble with the law. But for the vast majority of people, it doesn't make any sense. They ought to be very nervous about this conversation, and trying hard not to say the wrong thing. When being questioned by the police at work, how many people would really go nonchalantly about their business? It's a conundrum for the actor, because the director has instructed them to do something unrealistic. It's unwise to do the opposite of what the director tells you to do (more on that later), so unfortunately, that's the performance these poor actors have to give.

Listen and React. Having a point-of-view moment-to-moment is a direct result of another thing your acting teacher always said to you — "listen and react." When you hear something, show how it affects you, how it makes you feel (within reason, of course). I'm always looking for the moments when you realistically react to what just happened. A look on your face that shows you noticed that your spouse didn't respond to "I love you." Your anger upon hearing an insult. Your surprise at not being chosen for the plum assignment. The moment when you process new information, etc.

When an actor doesn't really listen to what another actor is saying, it's very clear. Then I'll be asked to find a take "where we can see the line land." In other words, find a take where the listener understands the importance of what has been said to them and reacts appropriately. That's a take where the line has landed on them.

Being in the moment and reacting is a hallmark of all the great actors I've edited. I can always count on them for a great reaction shot because they're so in the moment.

If you can be the actor in the scene who is always in the moment, listening and reacting to what's happening, you'll quickly become the actor that we editors look to for a good reaction when we need to highlight a moment. We will cut to you! Soon word will get around, and our regular directors will learn to cover you because you'll provide those moments for them.

Understand the cause and effect. Somebody has just said something to you, which makes you react in certain way. Why are you reacting that way? What is it about what they've just said that's causing you to do what you do next? The script lays out the outline of the action, but part of your job as an actor is to know "why" on a second-by-second level.

When I'm cutting a scene, I'm constantly asking "why?" What motivated these actions, this dialogue, at this precise second? The answer is almost always "because the other character said or did (something)." When an actor analyzes a script, you start with the big picture, then slowly work your way down to the beat-by-beat moments. As an editor, I'm looking at the scene and doing the same thing, down to the level of microbeats in the space between lines. And hopefully, when I'm replaying your takes over and over again in the cutting room, I'm going to see the results of your hard work. I'm going to see you living that experience in the moment and organically coming to every action that the script calls for you to perform.

Everything that happens in the story occurs as a result of something that happened before, whether it was one second ago or ten minutes ago. So understanding why you are doing or saying things really enhances your performance.

Be specific. This ties into point-of-view and listen / react. You are playing a specific reaction to a specific stimulus. Being emotional and crying may be fun for an actor, but it needs to communicate something very specific to the audience. For example, if Elaine began crying at the table after "Just say it. I want to hear you say it," would that be because...

- she knows she's about to do something terrible (murder Joe) which will change her life forever?

- she is angry at herself for getting into this situation?

- she is just hopeless?

All three choices are valid, but the director and writer are likely to have only one of them in mind. So you must choose one and convey it. If the audience can't tell what the crying means, then the crying is not very useful. They won't know what it means if the actor doesn't know either. So always be specific. Why do you do what you do? And what are you communicating through that action?

Remember the end of *Nell*? All of Nell's friends are reuniting at her lakeside cabin for a picnic. She plays happily with the young daughter of Liam Neeson and Natasha Richardson. When the little girl walks away, there's an incredible moment where Nell's face collapses and she is overwhelmed with emotion. The audience knows exactly why Nell is overwhelmed. She isn't crying because she loves her new life. She isn't crying because her legal troubles are over. She's crying because she misses her dead sister. Jodie Foster is very specific in her intention, so the audience reads her perfectly.

Know and show your previous given circumstances. Know where your character is coming from and what they have experienced. What was happening to you the moment before you walked through the door? The hour before you walked through the door? Where are you going? What do you expect to happen (or expect to find) when you get there? This can get a bit mind-bending when you are shooting a show out of sequence (meaning you shoot scene 10 before scene 9) but it's crucial for you to stay on top of it.

Every actor, no matter how talented, should be asking themselves these questions. On *The Shield*, when Glenn Close walked onto the set, she'd usually confer with the director about the same three questions: "What just happened? What time of day is it? Where are we in the story?" Sometimes she'd follow up the last question with "Do I know _____ yet?" (such as, "Do I know yet that he is the murderer?")

Characters come from one place, and go to another place, with a real goal in mind.

WHY WE SHOOT OUT OF SEQUENCE

We don't start filming with the first scene and then work our way in order to the last scene. Instead, the shooting order is jumbled. The scheduling decisions are usually based on two factors.

First, we want to group all of the scenes that take place at a certain location together, thus saving on the cost of renting the location multiple times. Second, since many actors are paid a daily rate, production tries to schedule all of a guest actor's scenes to be shot on the same day to avoid paying them for multiple days.

For example — near the end of *The Empire Strikes Back*, Luke Skywalker leaves his training with Yoda to rescue his friends in Cloud City. Once there, he enters the dimly-lit carbon freeze chamber. Before filming this scene, the actor should ask himself:

- Where am I coming from? *Sneaking through hallways looking for my imperiled friends, shot at by stormtroopers, and I was just warned by Leia that it's a trap.*

- Where am I going? *Into a dark room that I've never been in before.*

- What do I expect to find? *Some sort of trap. Possibly my enemy Darth Vader.*

- What do I think will happen? *A difficult fight, probably against Darth Vader, which I'm not sure I can win.*

We should see all of this on Luke's face and in his demeanor from the very first frame of the scene. I'm asking myself these questions before I start cutting the scene, so I'm looking for the answers on the actors' faces when I start watching their takes.

Occasionally I see problems where the actor is not bringing his emotion and experiences from the previous scene into the current one. If a character has been put through a very emotional scene, in the next scene I'd expect to see him still processing that experience. If he begins the second scene behaving happy and normal, that's problematic. I remember an instance where I had this situation in my dailies, and we solved it by cutting out the beginning of the second scene to avoid the part where the actor was clearly NOT processing the trauma of the previous scene. From an editing standpoint, the transition between the scenes was a bit clunky, but it's better than the strange disconnect between scenes that would exist if we had left everything intact.

You (as your character) really need to be living the experience, from the moment you walk through the door.

Know where your character is in the larger story. Smart actors know what their overall story arc is, and understand where each of their scenes fall on that continuum. That's why Glenn Close knew it was important to be sure of "Where are we in the story?" At the end of *Empire,* Luke does not behave the same way he did at the beginning of the film. His Jedi training has given him confidence and some patience. So Mark Hamill needed to play Luke differently, depending on whether he was doing a scene earlier in the film or later in the film.

Simple performances are usually the best — because they are usually the most honest. The most common request I hear in the cutting room from producers and directors is "Do you have a simpler version of that?" The camera enhances everything you do, so you don't have to over-exaggerate for your intention to come across. You can film yourself to see how things read. Notice that when you are more still, it's usually more powerful. The tendency to over-exaggerate is commonly called "being too theatrical," referring to the days when actors on stage had to overact to be understood by the audience in the back rows of the theater. If someone says that about your performance, it's not a compliment.

Let your character resist tears and shield their emotions. We almost never use the big, emotional, crying performances. Instead, we always go for the take where the actor is fighting back the tears. Think of Robert De Niro in *Silver Linings Playbook*. There's a great scene around 1 hour 13 minutes where he goes up to the attic and sits on his son Bradley Cooper's bed to talk to him about "Eagles luck." De Niro is quiet and simple, not big and exaggerated, so when the tears come, they feel natural, unforced, and not terribly welcome. As a result, the scene is heartbreaking. Another example is Emma Thompson in *Love Actually*, when she begins crying as she's listening to the Joni Mitchell CD her husband gave her for Christmas.

The same idea applies to anger. Watch well-directed movies and TV shows and see how often actors express anger with an intense, quiet delivery instead of furious shouting. It's almost always more interesting to watch someone trying to hide or suppress a big emotion than it is to watch them express the big emotion unshielded.

Show restraint. Another common complaint from producers and directors is that that actors are "too arch" or "mustache twirling." Usually this applies to actors playing bad guys or antagonists. Often the actor has triggered this critique by playing the character in a gleefully malicious or sadistic way — evil for evil's sake. Keep in mind that from your character's point-of-view, you're not an evil person. You're doing something that seems right or necessary to your character. So don't overdo it and become a caricature of a "bad guy."

Joe probably isn't blackmailing Elaine because he gets off on seeing a woman in distress. He's doing it because he needs the money and saw an opportunity. In fact, the scene might be more interesting if we saw that under his bravado, Joe felt bad about blackmailing her. That's a much better scene than one where Joe's objective is to take delight in Elaine's suffering.

Behaving the way you think a stereotypical bad guy behaves indicates that you're perceiving your character from the vantage point of other characters, when instead you should be inhabiting your character from the inside. Be an advocate for your character by grounding them in realistic behavior. Be a real person doing a real thing, regardless of whether the story views you as a bad guy.

Show your moment of decision. When cutting a scene, I am always very interested in seeing the beat where the character decides to do something. I call this the "moment of decision." The script presents the character with a choice or opportunity, and the character decides what to do.

For example, you're a cop and the District Attorney wants you to lie on the stand to save the case. I want to see you **decide** to do the DA's bidding, instead of seeing you simply **agreeing** to do his bidding. The moment of decision could also be for something much smaller — such as deciding to finally answer that phone which has been ringing during your conversation. It doesn't have to be a world-changing moment. What's important is that we see the beat of deciding.

I'm always looking for this moment, because it answers the audience's question "Why did they do that?" I like to see you come to an internal conclusion about what you're going to do. Otherwise, your character seems to change their mind and act for no honest reason.

In *Blackmailed Beauty*, there's a small moment of decision when Elaine decides to drink the coffee. Of course, the biggest one is before "Just say it," when Elaine decides that Joe's answer will determine whether or not she's going to kill him.

I also like to see the moments when a character decides to switch strategies and pursue a different way of getting what she wants. For example, when you can see an actor think, "Being nice to this guy isn't working, so now I'll try bullying him instead." You'll know you are being asked to show your moments of decision and reaction when a director tells you, "I want to see your gears turning."

Take the time that your character has earned to express this moment of decision, but remember, if you're not a lead character, the audience is probably not interested in watching a full minute of you agonizing over a choice. Decisive characters will decide quickly. Flaky characters go back and forth. But if this choice is not the point of the story, then don't milk it. I'm OK with five seconds on the CIA agent who's deciding to give the secret information to the terrorists so they don't kill his wife. But I'm not OK with five seconds on the face of a customer who's deciding that the cashier is too rude and now he's going to leave. Whether your reaction is big or small, remember — never go bigger than what your character has earned in the larger tapestry of the story. In *Sophie's Choice*, Meryl Streep made her life-altering choice in less than two seconds. Keep it real!

Act like this is the first time this ever happened. Your character doesn't know what's going to happen to him or her. A lot of the fun of watching actors on screen is seeing them get caught by surprise and then react. They didn't know this crazy thing would happen — whether it's the murderer jumping out of a closet, the Iron Man suit taking flight, or their husband saying "I'm leaving you." If you anticipate the thing you're not supposed to know is going to happen, these moments will disappear, and so will much of the fun of the scene. Let it all happen for the first time in every take. (I don't know how actors manage to keep being convincingly surprised take after take. That's an incredible skill!)

Your performance should have an arc in each scene, just like there is an arc in the larger story. For instance, in *Blackmailed Beauty*, Elaine could begin the scene unsure of what she is going to do about Joe. Over the course of the scene, as she realizes Joe will never let her out from his grip, Elaine's resolve grows, and finally she shoots him. So her arc could be moving from uncertainty to resolve. That's much more interesting to watch than the version of the scene where Elaine comes in completely committed to shooting Joe, and at the end of the scene, she does shoot him. In the cutting room, we'd say that this choice left her with "nowhere to go" — she's already arrived at the end point of her emotion at the beginning of the scene, so there is no change by the end. We might also say she's "playing the end of the scene." I'd likely get a note to "give her an arc." I'd try to address that note by looking for takes where Elaine appears less determined at the beginning of the scene.

A similar editorial note is being asked to "**modulate**" someone's performance. This means to add more nuance and emotional change. You can also think of it as changing where the character is on the emotional spectrum. If a character begins the scene angry and stays angry, there's not much growth. There's also nowhere for the angry actor to go when the other characters raise the stakes. So you need to modulate your performance. When this term is used, it usually means to reduce the intensity of the emotion. We can help modulate in the cutting room by using a "less angry" take for the first half and a "more angry" take for the last half. But you could modulate within your take on set, and then your emotional transition would be more organic.

Don't be thrown if the director directs you through a **range of performances**. Sometimes she's not sure just how emotional you should be, so she'll ask for something different each take. She may want a few different points on the spectrum. Maybe before take 1, the director will tell you that getting tripped by the office bully is annoying. Then before take 2, she'll tell you that getting tripped is the final straw for you, and you should become explosively angry. The director is trying to see what's right for your character. They are also evaluating the effect of your choices on the other characters in the scene. The director will probably settle on one interpretation fairly quickly (after all, she came to set with something in mind). But a good TV director knows that she doesn't have final cut. She's aware that after she's done editing, the showrunner will come in for his turn, and might ask me if there is a different take available with more or less emotion than the one the director picked. By providing a range of performances, the director gives us the material we need to experiment with variations of the scene. It will also let us address the inevitable studio and network notes that will come later: "Do you have a take where she's more _____?" "Did the director get one where he's less _____?"

We often combine pieces of the different performances to create the final performance. In the pilot of *Homeland*, there's a scene around 16 minutes 26 seconds where Brody reunites with his family for the first time after eight terrible years as a POW. Discussions between showrunner/creator Alex Gansa, director Michael Cuesta, and actor Damian Lewis (who won an Emmy that season for playing Brody), resulted in three takes on Damian for the moment where he sees his family, all of which expressed different ideas.

In take 1, Brody is delighted to see his family, makes eye contact, and smiles broadly as soon as he sees them. He embraces them warmly and his eyes tear up. In take 2, Brody is completely shut down. He's so damaged that he has no idea how to react to his family. Maybe he's not even sure they are real. He can't make prolonged eye contact and seems completely withdrawn. In take 3, Damian did a performance that was in-between the extremes of takes 1 and 2.

How this scene should be played was a subject of much discussion in the cutting room. Many of us felt that take 2, the "damaged" take, was the most interesting and the most realistic, although it ran counter to the happy homecoming that the audience wanted to see. The finished version is a combination of pieces from all three takes. When Brody first sees his family, we used the damaged take, and we stay in that performance until Brody's wife embraces him. Then I started using the warmer takes, and I didn't use take 1 until Brody spoke to his teenage daughter for the first time. Having three very different takes was extremely valuable for us. Please note, the choice to do this was made on set in conjunction with the director and showrunner. The actor shouldn't be doing something dramatically different in each take unless the director asks them to, otherwise none of the takes will cut together properly.

Put a button on the end of your scene. The button is the very last moment of the scene. You've seen it a million times in cop shows — the police are questioning a suspect, he slips up and admits he was at the scene of the crime, then the cops look at each other as if to say "now we've got him." It's an emotional response that "buttons up" the scene, a last little beat that clearly conveys the nature of the scene's resolution to the audience. It can be a look between two people, it can be the expression on the face of one character who knows he just got his objective... or it could be a look of "I just got away with it." Figure out your button and hold it. Don't dilute it with extraneous movements and gestures. Just clearly convey your end emotion.

When you watch a scene that doesn't have a button, all the energy and stakes in the scene seem to evaporate. You get a sense that none of the characters care about what just happened, or even registered what just happened. And if nothing significant happened, why did the scene exist in the first place? So there needs to be something. In *Blackmailed Beauty,* the button would be the look on Elaine's face right after she unloads her gun into Joe. Is she happy? Terrified? Devastated? Whatever choice is made, that's the button.

> ### ACTS IN TELEVISION
>
> The chunks of show between commercial breaks are called Acts.
>
> The part of the show before the opening Title Sequence, which needs to hook viewers into the show, is sometimes referred to as the "Teaser" or "Cold Open." The remaining acts are referred to by number: Act 1, Act 2, Act 3, Act 4.

If you want to see buttons in action, watch the last moment of a TV show right before a commercial break. That moment is called the "Act Out" and it's sort of a super-button. Not only does it button up the scene, but it's also a mini-climax strong enough to make the audience hang on through the commercials.

Forget about vanity. I always prefer the takes where you have the least physical dignity, because it means you are being the most honest. When I was cutting *The Shield,* I loved using the takes where Michael Chiklis got so worked up as Vic Mackey that you could see flecks of spittle fly out of his mouth when he yelled. It felt so real to me, how could I resist using it? When I cut *Homeland,* I love watching how Claire Danes' face trembles into the now famous "Claire Danes cry face." She turns red and begins to vibrate with emotion — she's not worrying about her dignity, she's living the moment. I like the post-coital takes where you don't look like you just came out of the makeup trailer, instead you're rumpled, your hair is a mess, and you look like a real person. The more real you are, the more I like it. Lauren Cohan, who plays Maggie on *The Walking Dead*, explained this perfectly in a 2013 issue of Emmy magazine: "When you're not worried about hiding flaws, it lets you go to better places emotionally."

CHAPTER 6

WHAT YOU CAN CONTROL:
YOUR TECHNICAL SKILLS

Great acting is not easy; anyone who says it is, is either shallow
or a charlatan. And one of the hardest things about acting
is admitting that it is hard.

— *Robert Cohen*

By mastering your technical skills, you can avoid the mistakes that force us to cut actors out.

Know your lines. If you're saying the wrong words, I can't put you on camera. And you will grievously offend the writers, who are the most powerful people in television, the ones with the power to say to me, "Get rid of that actor."

Every line has a carefully crafted meaning, and when you garble the words, the meaning is lost. When you forget words or sentences, important ideas or linkages are lost. Even if they seem unimportant in this scene, the lost words may set up future conflicts and interactions. If you add new words, you dilute the clarity of what's been written. Some actors think it's permissible to improvise as long as they get close to the meaning of the line. No way. When you go off book, there's a potential for huge problems. Your rewritten line might not include the phrase that your scene partner responds to, so now his line doesn't make any sense. Intentional or not, your rewrite could completely change the meaning of the scene, or alter the previous given circumstances. It might not sound right coming from the character you're playing, because you've changed the character's voice. It could introduce extraneous ideas that distract from the central idea of the scene. Worst of all, it could leave out an important detail that makes the story work, or confuse the plot of the whole story. In short — stick with the script!

If you absolutely can't get a line out because the grammar just won't come out of your mouth, politely sidebar with the director and they'll talk to the on-set writer about changing it in a way that keeps the intended meaning.

If you don't know your lines, your performance will probably be hesitant and you'll be adding pauses where there shouldn't be any. You're likely to be adding "um"s and "uh"s, which I will need to cut out because they make your character look uncertain. Then I'll be asked by directors and producers for a take where "the actor looks like they know their lines." Most of the audience doesn't realize which pauses are caused by an actor forgetting their lines and which pauses are for dramatic effect... but editors, directors, and producers are all very attuned to the difference. We will cut away from you to remove pauses. Please don't make us do that!

How does the editor get around the mistake of an actor saying the wrong lines? Unfortunately, every solution requires taking you off camera:

Option 1: I can try to "Frankenstein" the correct line together by combining bits of your dialogue from different takes. Hopefully I'll end up with a reading that sounds like a real sentence. But to cover my audio edits, I will have to cut to another actor during your line.

Option 2: If Frankenstein-ing doesn't work, then I'll record myself saying the correct line in my editing room. I'll cut that temp audio in, and we'll bring you in to an ADR booth later in the process to re-record your dialogue for real. But to cover your new audio, I'll have to cut to someone else so the audience doesn't see that your on-camera mouth doesn't match what they are hearing. Recording your ADR costs the production time and money, which doesn't make anyone happy.

Option 3: My final choice is to cut your line out altogether because your wrong words don't make any sense. If the scene works without your dialogue, then that becomes the easiest choice.

Note that all of my options result in the audience watching someone else when they should be watching you. Not ideal for your or me.

ADR

ADR is shorthand for "Additional Dialogue Recording". It's when we record (or re-record) dialogue after the show has finished shooting. We may be re-recording your on-set lines because the original recording was mechanically faulty, or because your performance wasn't right. Or the writers may add new lines for you to say because they feel plot points need to be made clearer.

You are brought into a special ADR room, where the section that needs a fix is played for you several times on a big screen. You rehearse to picture until you get the hang of it. Then we do a countdown and you perform your lines into the mic.

If you flub your line, where should you restart your dialogue? If you mess up a line in the middle of a take, that's OK. It happens. Often when an actor flubs her line, she will say in the moment, "I'm going to take that again, from when I stand up," or she'll say to the other actor, "Give me that [cue] again," and all the other actors understand what's about to happen. They hold their emotional space and the flubber does the line again (hopefully, this time saying the correct line). Everyone knows what it's like to mess up and nobody wants to make the other actor feel bad.

When flubbing, many actors will immediately correct themselves by repeating the right scripted word, and then press on. Unfortunately, that doesn't help me much, because they've restarted in the middle of a sentence. I want to keep your complete thought and action on camera — ideally including the emotional moment that led your character to say the dialogue — so I'd like you to start from the beginning of the sentence, or maybe even the beginning of that block of dialogue.

On set, the director will usually yell out where to restart from if they see you are having trouble, but if you are restarting yourself, then please remember — start back at the emotion that led to this beat.

After Elaine hears Joe say, "I own you," she stands up and says, "You bastard, you've ruined my life. You pushed and pushed and now I don't have a choice." Then she shoots Joe. If Elaine forgets her dialogue halfway through "You pushed and pushed," it's best if she starts over from the last beat of the sitting position, because I want to show her decide to stand up and say her dialogue without having to cut away from her.

Don't restart from here.   Restart from here.

If returning to the previous physical position is not possible, then Elaine should start from the very beginning of her line when standing — "You bastard".

When you restart in the middle of an idea, it reduces my choices. Just because I'm an editor doesn't mean I want to cut all over the place — it's often more compelling to see everything unfold.

If you sit back down, or otherwise return to a previous physical position, the camera crew will need a chance to readjust framing and focus. Give them the few seconds they need, or else you'll be out of focus when you start up again. When the director sees that the cameras are ready, he should call "action" again to indicate you should resume.

If the cameras are behind you, looking at your scene partner over your shoulder, it's OK if you didn't deliver your line 100% perfectly, so long as you convey the right idea and say it in the same amount of time. I probably wasn't going to use your audio anyway — I was going to steal the audio from your best on-camera take. So you don't need to break the momentum of the scene to correct yourself if you're not on-camera.

In summary, start over at a logical place and repeat an action if needed.

Physical continuity is critical. Irrelevant on stage, but crucial to on-camera acting, continuity means performing the same physical actions *identically* in every take. That's noting when you move, when you stop moving, how you move, and matching that action in every take. For example, note at which point in the dialogue you turn around to face someone, which hand you use to pass your scene partner a folder, when you lean back in your chair, when you touch your face, etc.

If you reached for your soda can *before* saying, "I need a drink," in take 1, then you have to match this choreography in every other take. You must always do it in the same order, because I'm editing the scene together using multiple angles and takes, and the action in all of them needs to match. You can't change the sequence of events in take 3 by reaching for the can *after* saying, "I need a drink." That's not going to cut together with your other takes—or your scene partner's takes. The other actors are reacting to your actions, so if you move at the wrong time, their eyes will be looking in the wrong place. It's extremely important to be consistent, whether the camera is on you or on someone else. Then I'll always have the option to keep your best work in the scene.

Humans are hardwired to notice mismatching movements, so editors work hard to avoid them. The audience may not immediately recognize what doesn't match, but they will sense something is off. We don't want the audience to become distracted by a character's soda can inexplicably jumping from table to hand and back again between shots. To maintain the illusion of our fictional world, we need you to maintain continuity.

I want to cut every scene for the best performances, but when there are continuity problems, I'll have to use inferior takes just to hide the physical mismatch. Your worst performance might wind up on screen because that was the only take where continuity matched. Or I might have to cut away from you entirely until the mismatching action is over. That's how you end up on the cutting room floor.

This happened in a two person scene I cut. The

Drinker and the Listener were facing each other talking. The Drinker had a cup of coffee in his left hand. In his coverage, he said a provocative line and then drank the coffee. He drank at the same point in every take with his left hand. So far, so good. But when the camera moved behind him to film coverage of the other actor, the Drinker wasn't so vigilant. During the Listener's best take, the Drinker goofed and used his right hand to lift his coffee. That was the wrong hand. The mistake was clear.

Here's what that continuity mistake would look like in *Blackmailed Beauty*:

Joe's cup in left hand.   Joe's cup in **right** hand.

See how the coffee cup jumped hands?

Here's how it would look if Joe had done it correctly:

Joe's cup in left hand.   Joe's cup in left hand.

In the scene I was cutting, the obvious mismatch meant that I couldn't use the Listener's best reaction. So I had to use the Listener's second-best take — which was not nearly as good. Only because the Drinker's arm was a correct match. That's a change I really hated having to make for such a preventable reason.

Some actors complain that continuity is too rigid. They say it prevents them from being in the moment and producing an organic performance. "I can't be in the moment if I'm worrying about whether my glass is up or down!" My answer is simply that you have to learn this skill and make it part of your craft. If you give the most incredible performance, but your continuity is a disaster, we probably can't use that take. So the performance will wind up being useless after all. Keeping your continuity consistent lets the audience focus on the important things – like your performance.

Continuity is a very mechanical skill, but it's absolutely crucial. Actors who can't internalize their continuity get a troublesome reputation very quickly. Editors aren't shy about pointing out to showrunners that an actor's bad continuity is what forced us to use sub-par performances. We're hoping that if we mention it enough, someone will talk to the actor about what they're doing wrong, and the problem won't continue.

In episode 107 of *Homeland,* there's a scene where Mandy Patinkin is sitting in a booth at a diner across from his prisoner Aileen. The waitress (a day player) brings Mandy a plate of burger and fries. She puts it down in front of him with the burger facing the wall and the fries facing the aisle.

The crew began filming the scene with the wide shots. Then they moved in to shoot coverage. In every take, the waitress put the plate down with the burger facing the wall and the fries facing the aisle.

In take 1 of Mandy's medium shot, the waitress made a continuity error and put the plate in front of Mandy backwards — so the burger was facing the aisle. Mandy caught the mistake instantly. He turned the plate the correct way, then asked the actress playing the waitress to pick it up again, step off camera, then come back in and lay the plate down the right way as if she's just arrived with the food. She did it, and they continued the scene as if nothing had gone wrong.

Mandy saved the take. If he hadn't fixed the mistake, I wouldn't have been able to use any of what followed because the plate continuity was wrong. Every time I cut from that take to another take, the food would appear to have turned around, which would be tremendously distracting.

Each actor is responsible for their own continuity. You shouldn't be spending energy keeping track of every tiny detail of what all the other actors are doing. You only need to be concerned with what affects you. I'm sure that Mandy wasn't trying to be the continuity policeman. He probably noticed the problem because he was supposed to snack on the fries using his left hand. When Mandy looked down and realized the fries were in the wrong place, he knew his own continuity was going to be wrong, so he made the fix.

Mandy Patinkin can get away with occasionally correcting other actors' continuity, but if you're a day player with only two lines, you're in a very different situation.

This story demonstrates something that always amazes me about actors. You have the ability to live rich emotional moments virtually on demand, but even in the midst of those moments, there is a still a part of your brain that can focus on the technical things like continuity without diminishing your emotional performance. I find that truly incredible.

Hit your marks. The camera crew needs to know where you are going to be standing so they can set their lenses to the right focus point. The exact place where you will be standing is your "mark." Often this will be marked for you on the floor with a piece of colored tape. If you're not on the mark... you're out of focus. The camera crew will try to adjust if you land in the wrong place, but High Definition cameras are not very forgiving, so the focus pullers don't have much wiggle room. It's your responsibility to be where you are supposed to be. Remember — if you are not in focus, I can't cut to you.

Elaine is on her mark, in clear focus.

Elaine is off her mark. She's blurry — so I can't use the take.

And because she's in a different position in the frame, I can't mix this with other takes where she's in the right place.

Develop the skill of landing on a mark without looking like you're landing on a mark. Make it appear natural that you stopped there. In real life, people don't look at the ground for the mark that tells them where to stop. They also don't stop at a random place in the room so they can turn into a nice over-the-shoulder shot. They stop for natural reasons. Figure out what's motivating you to stop (or turn, or whatever) so it looks real when you do it. Because it is noticeably fake when you don't.

Say your lines in the same places when doing walk-and-talk shots or going up and down stairwells. If you've ever seen an episode of *The West Wing*, you've seen a walk-and-talk. It's the shot where the camera is in front of or alongside the actors as they walk through the busy set, talking a mile a minute, passing all sorts of interesting set decoration and background actors. If you're on the move and greatly vary the pace of your dialogue from take to take, when the scene is cut together the audience may notice that you seem to pass the same people and objects multiple times. That's because we're cutting between takes where you passed things at different points in the dialogue.

You especially can't get away with it on a staircase, because every time you turn a corner, it sends a clear signal to the viewers about your physical location. The potential problem occurs if you start or finish a line several stairs away from where you said it in previous takes. When the editor combines that take with other takes, you may appear to suddenly teleport from the middle of the stairs to the bottom, or appear to round a corner twice. Or, the person you are talking to doesn't match her previous shot because now she's reacting while occupying a different location in the stairwell. The editor is forced to cut the scene for continuity instead of for performance, and your best take may not get used. To avoid this common problem, you should say your lines in the same places on the stairwell every time.

Connect the ideas in your dialogue. Pausing in the wrong place breaks up the ideas in the writing and thus reduces clarity. Don't pause in the middle of an idea. Keep things connected. If you don't understand what your line means, then please ask the director on the day, and they will be glad to explain it to you. That's much better than you trying to bluff your way through it and fooling nobody. If you don't understand what you are saying (or why you're saying it), then the audience probably won't either... and we'll have to cut it out.

Don't overlap dialogue with other actors in the scene. We overlap other people in real life all the time, cutting them off or talking over them. Overlapping says a lot about our emotional state. But it is a problem on camera. I want to use your best take of each of your lines. I also want to use your scene partner's best take of their lines. But we probably didn't shoot the best performance of both actors simultaneously. You got four takes with the cameras pointed at you, and then she got four takes with cameras on her. Maybe you were best in take 1, and your partner was best in take 2. If there is no overlapping, I can easily cut between those takes. But if you speak over each other, then all the dialogue is married together, and I can't cut between takes easily. If it was her best performance, but you overlapped with your worst performance, I can do some fancy audio editing to try to solve the problem, but it would be much better if the problem didn't exist in the first place. My ideal scenario is to have your best take with clean audio, and her best take with clean audio. Then I can use everyone's best work, and I can create the overlap in the cutting room, where it's easy to control which takes overlap and how much. The big exception to this rule is if the director tells you to overlap on set. In that case, do it. The director is always the boss.

When the script calls for you to say part of a line that will get **cut off** by the next character, it's important that you know what your character would have said if they hadn't been cut off. Because sometimes the other actor doesn't say their line quickly enough, and you are left standing there looking silly, waiting to be cut off without anything else to say. You need to be prepared to keep talking if necessary. You should also know what your character was going to say so your performance conveys the right intention until you are cut off. You should know what you are saying even if the audience never hears you, because your performance will be their only clue. Even though it was inaudible to the audience, Bill Murray knew what he whispered to Scarlett Johansson at the end of *Lost In Translation*. It is only because of the intention of his performance (and Scarlett's reaction) that the audience is able to make a solid guess about what he might have said.

If your scene partner is late on their cue, don't break your demeanor. Stay in the moment and wait for them to remember. You don't know when the editor is going to cut from you to the other actor, or vice versa, and you limit our choices by making faces. I edited a scene where an actor was supposed to say a line and then immediately be tackled by a stuntman. The line came, but the stuntman was late on his cue and didn't tackle right away. The actor made a goofy face — "where is he?" — and *then* got tackled. I couldn't use any of it because the actor still had his goofy face on when he got hit. It would have been better if he just stayed in the moment and waited for the hit to come.

Know the style of the show you're working on. If possible, before your big day on set, you should watch an episode of the show you'll be acting in. You want to get an idea of the acting style so you can deliver what they are expecting. If someone shows up to work on *Homeland* but they perform as if they were on *Friends*, that's wrong and it's going to frustrate the director and other actors. It's best to have a good idea of what you're contributing to and how they do things, then calibrate yourself accordingly. In the cutting room, that kind of stylistic mismatch results in me getting the note that "this character seems like he's in a different movie."

Act at the right tempo. If you speak very slowly or react very slowly, and it's not appropriate for your character, I will have to cut to other actors to speed you up under their shots (that's called "pulling up the ʻalogue"). If you're taking forever, you're ruining the flow of things and you're going to get pulled up. That said, different actors in the same drama can (and should) move at different paces if it is appropriate for their characters. For example, Luke Skywalker speaks quickly, but Yoda speaks slowly. Likewise, different shows move at a different pace. There are virtually no pauses in *The Shield*, but there are lots of pauses in *Homeland*. So calibrate yourself appropriately to the show you are on.

If the pacing between the two actors is within the reasonable range, then we can play the scene in a shot that shows both actors. When the pacing is egregiously out of whack, then we're forced to go into coverage when we may not want to. I like seeing both people in a single shot when I can, but if I have to use close-ups earlier than I planned to avoid unnecessary and unwarranted pauses, then I will.

Regardless of your tempo, be sure that you are connecting ideas in your dialogue and are not leaving such large pauses that the meaning of the dialogue is lost.

React in some way during long speeches. When your scene partner is doing a long speech and you are the listener, be sure to really listen! We want to see what effect these words have on you. As mentioned earlier, I'm usually going to help the audience check in with the listener by cutting to you during a long speech. However, when I do so, you don't want to appear to be a completely motionless person. More than once I've been accused of cutting in a still image because the listener was so frozen. Act in the way that feels right, but just know that if you look away, or widen your eyes, or cock your head, or do any other action that shows your response to what you're hearing, it can be very helpful to the editor.

Look at what's important. What you look at tells the audience what you are interested in. Whether it's a person's face or an incoming missile, the audience always wants to know what you're looking at.

Editors take advantage of this by using the movement of an actor's eyes to motivate the cut from one shot to the next. "Follow the eyes," editors are told, which really means "show the audience what the actor is looking at." If you are having a conversation with two people, your eyes will naturally move from one person to the other as they take turns speaking. The editor will use your eye movement as a motivation to cut from you to the person speaking. If someone other than the person you are looking at begins to speak, you should look towards them (unless your character is making a choice not to look).

Humans always glance at (or move their bodies to look at) the source of an unexpected noise. Watch people around you and you will see this phenomenon in real life. Imagine that in *Blackmailed Beauty*, we're on a close-up of Elaine in the diner booth. When the Waitress begins to speak off-camera, the unexpected sound will cause Elaine look up at her. As soon as Elaine looks, the editor will cut to a shot of the Waitress. Elaine's eye movement motivates the cut. Just like Elaine, when your character hears unexpected sound, you should look for the source of the sound.

Watch some TV shows or movies with the sound turned off and pay attention to when the editor cuts. Notice how often the cut is motivated by someone's eye movement. Actors look, and the audience (and the editor) will follow.

If you're holding an important prop that you know will require a close-up, glance at it at the right time to create an opportunity for the editor to cut to the close-up. For example, you're a cop and you're holding a "wanted" flyer. The suspect is right in front of you, so you look from the suspect down to the flyer to compare faces — and that enables us to cut to the close-up of the flyer. Very helpful. Thank you, actor!

Similarly, if you are looking around the room for an object, your head and eye movements create an opportunity for us to cut to your point-of-view shot. Make sure to play the moment where you locate what you're looking for, because we're going to cut to your reaction after the POV shot.

In a Hitchcock movie, if you were the only character who knew there was a bomb hidden in the room, every time you glanced at the hiding place, we could cut to a shot of the bomb.

Maintain eye contact (or not). Once you get to the meaty part of a scene, you should try to maintain eye contact with your scene partner, assuming the blocking allows it and you haven't been told otherwise by the director or the script. Eye contact shows that your character is in the moment and deeply engrossed in whatever action is occurring. Often we select a take because the actors held eye contact longer then they did in the other takes.

It can be interesting to play with when you break eye contact, or whether you even allow eye contact. Avoiding eye contact shows fear, reluctance, evasion, or timidity. There is a great scene in the final episode of *The Shield* (at 54 minutes 55 seconds) where Detective Claudette Wyms (played by CCH Pounder) finally has dirty cop Vic Mackey (Michael Chiklis) in the interrogation room. After softening him up with some brutal accusations, Claudette takes graphic crime scene photos out of her manila folder and one by one, lays them down on the table in front of him. The photos are intended to break Mackey by showing him the consequences of his terrible choices. But Chiklis made a brilliant choice. He refused to even glance at the photos as CCH laid them out.

Instead, he maintained defiant eye contact with her, no matter how much she tried to make him look at the photos. Chiklis' refusal to look conveyed volumes about his character's feelings in that moment… and once CCH left the room and Chiklis did look down, his reaction was even more devastating because the audience knew he had been trying to avoid the moment. These are the kinds of fantastic choices you can make which will elevate the work.

Keep your face visible. Unless hiding your face serves a purpose in the scene, try to keep it visible so the audience can read your emotions. For example, when you're answering the phone, remember that the handset blocks one side of your face from view. Consider holding the phone in the hand that keeps your face clear for camera. If you're going to have your hands up by your face for a while, give a thought to which hand will block camera and which one won't.

Actresses need to adjust their long hair when it's blocking the face during a take. You lean down to look at a computer screen, and your hair falls past your ear and blocks your face. As soon as you can do it naturally, without looking like you are doing it for the benefit of the camera, please tuck that hair back and make your face visible. Claire Danes is a genius at readjusting her hair without drawing attention to it. You never get the sense that she's moving hair to keep camera happy. Even though this may seem like a silly detail, it's actually a big deal to us. If a curtain of hair keeps us from seeing the character's face for a long time, then that part of the take is no good. Audiences want to see faces.

Deal with your glasses only when you're likely to be on camera. Put them on (or take them off) just before your line, during your line, or right after you finish your line. Or you can remove them in reaction to something that was said to you. But don't randomly put them on or take them off in the middle of the other actor's dialogue. If I cut from that actor to you and you're suddenly wearing glasses that you didn't have on before, the audience will be jarred. To them, it will seem like the glasses have magically appeared on your face. I want to stay on the actor who is speaking for their entire line, so I don't want to interrupt the emotional flow of their work just for a quick shot that establishes you've put on your glasses. Respect the scene — and your fellow actor — by doing your glasses business when it's likely that you'll already be on screen.

Act beyond "Cut." Time seems to move differently on the set. When everyone is watching the scene live on monitors at the video village, the place where "Cut!" is called seems right. But the next day when we watch the footage in the cutting room, we often realize that we want the actors' final looks to continue for a few more beats. (That's a frequent note from network and studio executives: "Can you hold a beat longer on the end of this scene?") You don't have to stop acting the instant the director says "Cut," unless you're in an action scene or doing a dangerous stunt. If you're holding your look and buttoning the scene, just hold it a little longer after "Cut" and then be done. On most sets, the camera operators wait a few beats after hearing "Cut" before turning off the cameras, so if you continue acting, your extra moment will likely be recorded. I can easily remove the sound of "Cut!" and the crew talking, which allows me to keep holding on you for those additional beats. Believe me, your editor will appreciate the extra frames.

Be aware of when you blink. Walter Murch, a very influential editor and theorist, proposed a rule about when to cut away from an actor in his aptly named book *In the Blink of an Eye: A Perspective on Film Editing.* I follow it and it works. The rule is to always cut away on the frame before the actor blinks, because when a person is at the end of an emotion, they tend to blink. Watch the people around you in the real world and you'll notice this phenomenon. They will say, "I love you" (blink) — not "I love (blink) you."

Blinking ends an emotion. It also diminishes most emotions. When an actor says their line and then blinks several times, it creates a confusing impression. Rather than being a clear emotional moment, the intention becomes muddied. If you can control yourself at this deep level, try to be conscious of not letting yourself blink repeatedly unless the blinking itself is conveying a true emotion (such as confusion).

Make sure your diction is clear. We don't want to be forced to ADR what you said just because you mumbled and nobody could understand you. Your ADR performance won't be as good, and the new recording never exactly matches the sound of on-set production audio. We'd rather record your audio clearly and clean on set.

Be cognizant of when you do loud things. When you shut the door in the middle of someone's line (your line or someone else's), the sound of the door is usually so loud that it will drown out the actor's voice. Because the voice and the door overlap each other, they are married together and we can't control how loud one sound is in relation to the other. In situations like these, important dialogue often gets drowned out. It can happen with loud paper rustling, slamming down drinks, opening things, etc. Soon we're searching through the takes for audio where the actor's words are actually audible, instead of searching for the take where the actor's performance is best. If you can, try to shut the door between words or between lines, or else shut it softly. Use the same principle when slamming down your coffee cup or doing any other loud thing. Of course, you should be in the moment and do these things when it's right for your character. It's worse if you appear strangely hesitant to shut the door, just because you're waiting for the right moment to avoid drowning out a line. The rule is that when possible and when it appears natural, act in a way so as to avoid the overlap.

If you're using your own wardrobe, don't wear any clothing that has logos on it. Avoid anything with a graphic that could have been copyrighted — no logos, symbols, or images. That means no Nike logo, no Fighting Irish Norte Dame jersey, no Jimi-Hendrix-blowing-smoke T-shirt. Because copyright owners could object to the way their brand is being portrayed, the show's legal department will attempt to avoid lawsuits by preemptively seeking permission to use the logo (that's called "clearing" the logo). If the show provides you with wardrobe that has logos or imagery on it, you should assume the clearances have been granted. My concern is with clothing and accessories that you've brought from home to use as wardrobe on camera.

If you're filmed wearing a logo which hasn't been cleared, rather than run the risk of being sued, the show may just get rid of you instead. I worked on a episode where we had to delete an entire scene because a featured actor was wearing a baseball cap with a Major League Baseball team's logo on it. The actors were all good, and the scene was nice, but we couldn't cut around the guy's hat, and blurring the logo would have looked obvious and terrible.

Once we realized losing the scene wouldn't kill the story, it was a no-brainer to just remove it. I've always felt bad about that. The actor did a great job. It was the wardrobe department's fault because they should never have let him go on set wearing that hat. But it happened, and he got cut out.

Keep your hands out of your pockets when standing. Unless you are making a clear statement about your character or the script tells you to do it, take your hands out of your pockets! It shuts off your ability to express yourself physically.

When it's time to die, just die. Actors who are killed on screen, whether by gun, knife, electrocution, or whatever – please die quickly, unless the script requires otherwise. Obviously if you've got lines as you die ("just... go on... without me, boys...") then this doesn't apply, but if the script says, "Elaine shoots Joe. He dies. She flees," then we don't need twenty seconds of Joe gasping, choking, sliding down in his seat and slowly closing his eyes. If the moment of your death is the point of the scene ("I think he's trying to tell us who fired the shot! Let's lean closer!"), go ahead and milk it, but if the plot needs to race on past the moment, don't be a hammy roadblock.

I've watched many takes of actors dying slower than paint drying, and more than once I've heard the frustrated director yelling on set, "Die! Just die already!" Like he heard my own thoughts and shouted them out. My favorite time was the actor who'd been shot and while bleeding on the pavement, kept fighting for every last breath, each one more labored than the last, until finally he was rewarded with the furious director yelling in front of the entire crew, "Be dead! Just be dead!"

Keep your pen motionless. Fiddling with an object in a very distracting way pulls focus from both your face and the story. I cut a scene where the lead actor was listening intently to a long monologue delivered by the character across the table, a monologue that the lead was very interested in, yet the lead was slowly twirling a pen between his fingers the entire time. Motion attracts the eye, so the audience's attention kept jumping to the pen, when it should have been fixed on the emotions playing on the lead's face. Just as bad, the twirling suggested to the audience that the character wasn't really interested in what he was hearing, which was contrary to the point of the scene.

This problem occurred in another scene where a debate was taking place around a conference room table. When the argument between the two leads was heaviest, a background actor sitting behind them was twirling a pen in his fingers. It wasn't a character choice, because his character should have been very engaged in tracking the outcome of the debate. This actor was bored and not paying attention. How could I avoid the distraction? By using closer coverage on the foreground debater, framing out the pen twirler. Pulling focus from the leads to yourself in this manner is selfish and will ensure that ADs don't hire you for background work in the future.

Watch yourself on screen. I firmly believe that you need to see yourself on screen to understand how your work is coming across. You need to see how the camera magnifies everything, which will help you learn not to push too much. You can see if what you thought you were projecting is what the camera actually sees. I know some actors say, "Oh, I can't stand to see myself on film," but I think this attitude undermines the learning process. You should be capable of being analytical about yourself and watching your work with an objective attitude. It will help you enormously. I think you should seek out acting classes that film each session's scene work and give students a copy to take home with them. If you shoot something with your friends, ask them for a copy of the dailies so you can evaluate yourself. You can even film yourself with your phone if that's the only tool you've got. Just make sure you know what the rest of the world is seeing when you are performing.

CHAPTER 7

WHAT YOU CAN CONTROL:
YOUR ATTITUDE ON SET

If you want to gather honey, don't kick over the beehive.

— *Dale Carnegie*

When you book a role on a TV series, you're walking into an environment that has been humming along just fine without you. The crew has been working together season after season. The director is likely to have helmed previous episodes of the show. The cast regulars know their parts inside and out. **You are a guest in this family.** You need to act like one. **Be respectful.**

The most obvious way to be respectful is avoid being a diva. Be on time. Be friendly to everyone. Be a professional. Actors with an attitude are noticed and remembered for all the wrong reasons. Directors complain about them to the editors and producers. "That guy was really rude to the ADs." "She was late to set." Everyone makes a mental note: don't hire that actor again. Word travels fast. It can even get up to the bigwigs at the studio or the network, some of whom might have been on set that day and seen your bad behavior in person. Before you know it, you've burned your reputation... and your future prospects. Was bossing someone around to get you a coffee faster worth losing all that?

You will probably run into these crew members again in your career. Or they may tell bad things about you to their friends who work on other shows. Keep your reputation pristine — this is a small industry!

Listen to the director and do what they ask of you. You only know a small slice of the big pie you are working on — but the director knows every flake of the crust and every berry in the filling. He had an hours-long tone meeting with the showrunner before filming began, where they discussed every scene's meaning and goals. The director has the big picture. You don't. So when the director tells you how he wants the scene played, you need to listen to him and try to meet his vision. Of course you should advocate for your character, and try things to make it more interesting — but within reason. Because at the end of the day, if the director wanted red and you would only play green... he's going to try to cut you out of the show. From his point of view, the scene doesn't work solely because of you. He wants you out, not just because you ruined the scene, but also because you acted like a diva and didn't give him any performances that work. I've had directors say to me, "I kept telling him to do it the other way and he wouldn't get off it. Now we gotta get him out of the scene or the whole thing is ruined."

The director is worried about more than what your choices did to the quality of the drama. He's also worried about how your poor work reflects on him. In television, the director is work-for-hire, an employee whose job is to deliver the episode that the showrunner asks for. The showrunner is probably the person who first said "Play this scene red." When the director only brings back performances where you played green, and there are no choices or ways to make it red, it makes the showrunner question the director's competence... and maybe not want to hire him again. No director wants that!

If the director really disliked you on a personal level, he will probably try to reduce your screen time to a minimum. Every time he sees your face on screen, it reminds him of how awful it was to work with you. So he'll try to chop you out.

After the director is done being frustrated with you and heads off to his next show, the showrunner will come in for her cut, see what's happened to her brilliantly written scene and ask, "Why is it so choppy?" Then I'll say, "Because the actor sucked and we tried to cut around them." The showrunner will try to fix all the problems caused by the wrong performance, but may just give up and cut the scene out altogether. Next we'll send the show to the studio and the network, and they'll say, "What happened to that fun little scene?" Or worse... "What happened to that scene where we find out why the killer did it? It feels clipped short now." The showrunner will say, "The actor was not good. That's the best we can do." Now the studio and network bigwigs know you were awful! They have input on casting for all of the shows that they air. You can be sure that they will try to avoid using you in the future.

All because you thought your interpretation was better than the director's. Was it worth it?

CHAPTER 8

WHAT YOU CAN'T CONTROL:
BEING CUT OUT BECAUSE OF STORY OR TIME

I am a member of a team, and I rely on the team,
I defer to it and sacrifice for it, because
the team, not the individual, is the ultimate champion.

— *Mia Hamm*

Actors think that the biggest reason they wind up on the cutting room floor is because they were bad. But that's not really true. It's actually very common for an actor's scene to be cut out due to running time considerations, or because the scene wasn't needed for the story.

Scripts are usually written a little longer than the estimated final length of the show, because there will always be some scenes and moments that don't work well. Once those bits get cut out, there still needs to be enough show to meet the minimum running time. Hence the longer scripts.

In Post Production we are usually fighting the opposite battle — trying to get our show down to the maximum allowable running time. The network won't let us broadcast an episode that's too long because it eats into the time they're selling for commercials, which is where they make the bulk of their money. Movie studios dislike long films because they reduce the number of screenings that a theater can sell each day. So we must get the show "to time."

Often the Editor's Cut is ten minutes too long, because we've included every line, every beat, and every moment for the director to see. The Director's Cut is usually three to seven minutes over. Producers' Cut is where the big deletions happen. We call this process "tightening" or "getting to time."

First we cut out unnecessary pauses and shots of people entering or exiting rooms. We start looking for lines of dialogue we can eliminate ("line lifts"). We take the back end off any scene that's playing past the moment. We also remove scenes (and parts of scenes) that aren't totally necessary to make the show work.

Along with cutting lines that are poorly performed or don't land properly, we often lift lines that take the scene off track. If the scene is two managers deciding whether to fire the protagonist, we don't really need the section where the managers also discuss their favorite pop song. Eliminating those lines keeps the focus on the firing, which is the main point of the scene.

Let's say that there's another scene in the script for *Blackmailed Beauty*, one that takes place right before the big confrontation. In this new scene, we see Elaine drive up to the diner. Because the story is set in Los Angeles, Elaine has to valet her car when she arrives at the parking lot. So the scene is: Elaine pulls up, the valet opens her door, she gets out. The valet says, "Keys please." Elaine hands him the keys, he gives her a valet receipt. She says "Thank you," puts the receipt in her purse, and walks into the diner.

Do we really need this twenty second scene? Isn't the story better if we don't bother with Elaine valeting the car? If we just start with Elaine entering the diner, then we can cut out twenty seconds. That gets us closer to time. Now I won't have to cut twenty seconds of meaningful pauses out of the scene inside where she confronts Joe. Best of all, removing the valet scene helps move the story along. But the poor actor who played the valet winds up on the cutting room floor. I feel badly about making these sorts of suggestions to producers and directors, but they are very necessary. We need to preserve the core of our story, and everything else must fall to the wayside.

The Golden Rule is: If a scene slows down or derails the flow of the story, it needs to be recut or removed.

Another common scenario is having a really good scene that plays in the wrong place. For example, Elaine decides she's going to go confront Joe. But first she goes to her sister's house and drops off her will in case she loses the gunfight. The scene with the sister is very good, but it completely stops the momentum of the story. All the tension and pacing we're building up grinds to a halt for this drawn-out scene that the audience doesn't really need to see in the first place. The audience is screaming for the confrontation with Joe. So why are we wasting time with this scene? If we cut it, the story keeps moving in an interesting, compelling way. If we keep it, everything withers. That's a pretty easy choice to make in the cutting room. Once you get rid of everything that's not essential, what's left behind shines even brighter.

As Shawn Ryan often says, "Editing is the final stage of screenwriting." It's the part of the process where you learn what your story is really about, and then tailor everything to tell that story in the best way possible.

In police shows, we often find that it's not necessary to completely spell out the steps our hero detectives take to get from Point A to Point C. Sometimes we can cut a scene where they talk to a witness and it's still plausible that they got the information which leads them to the next location. Unfortunately, that means cutting out the actor who played the witness, even though they did a fine job.

It will help you to always remember that the main characters of the show are the characters that the show is most interested in. Everyone else is playing a supporting part. You are one of many factors in a scene. Although that scene is the most important thing in your world, it may not be most important thing in the story. Editors serve the story first, not the actors first. Ultimately, *Blackmailed Beauty* is about the blackmailer and his victim. That is the story of this movie. It is not about the valet, the Waitress, or Elaine's sister.

If you are playing a part that revolves around the main characters and you get cut, keep that truism in mind. As you work longer in the business, you will move up the ranks from one-line co-star to series regular. But even when you get to the top your work can still be cut for time or pacing, because at the end of the day, it's all about the story.

There are many famous examples of scenes that were cut from movies, and these days you can often see them in the "extras" section of DVDs and Blu-rays. Most TV shows also include deleted scenes on their season box sets or post them online after an episode airs. On *The Shield*, Shawn Ryan would usually record a special commentary track for deleted scenes that explained why the scenes were eliminated, and he often praised the actors for their performances. You can get the DVDs and judge for yourself if the scenes work on their own. But for editors, what's more important is how well the scenes work in the larger context of the story. (By the way, listening to the commentary tracks on DVDs is an excellent way for you to gain insight on how other members of the creative team make their decisions.)

CHAPTER 9

HOW TO BE A GOOD
BACKGROUND ACTOR

Don't be afraid to give your best to what seemingly
are small jobs. Every time you conquer one
it makes you that much stronger. If you do the little jobs well,
the big ones will tend to take care of themselves.

— *Dale Carnegie*

If you are a background actor, the most important thing to realize is that you are not the main story in this scene. Your mantra should be: "Don't draw attention away from the leads." It is your job to convince the audience that this scene is taking place in a real world environment. Everything beyond that is the job of the other actors.

Even as a background actor, anything you do that breaks the illusion of the world that the show is trying to create will make an editor want to cut you out. So being able to act natural, regardless of the environment of the scene, is the most important skill to have.

Background actors who go wrong usually fall into one of two camps. They are either over-actors or under-actors.

Over-actors try to call attention to themselves. While the leads are performing their scene at the foreground table in the restaurant, over-actors at the background tables gesticulate wildly to each other, as if they can only communicate using crazy body language. They laugh outrageously, they stumble over invisible objects, they over-emphasize everything. In short, they're distracting, and my strategy for cutting the scene quickly becomes about how much I can keep them off screen.

Meanwhile, under-actors have no sense that they are in a real, functioning world. Content in their cocoon, they do fine until the bomb explodes at the table next to them — and then they don't react. Two men start throwing punches in the line for the bathroom and the under-actors behind them don't seem to notice a thing. Once again, cutting the scene becomes about keeping these people off screen, because they are ruining the illusion that everyone else in the show is trying so hard to create.

There's a fine line between appropriate reactions and overacting. You want to respond to what's happening in your environment in an authentic way that helps tell and serve the story, while avoiding being so grandiose that you draw attention away from the leads and onto yourself. Stay on the correct side of this line and you'll stay in the show.

The opposite way to do it? Get yourself a copy of the original *Ghostbusters* and go to around 1 hour, 19 minutes, 40 seconds. At this point in the story, the Ghostbusters' containment system has been shut down and ghosts are running rampant through the city. Crowds of people are gathered outside Sigourney Weaver's apartment building, staring up at the menacing black cloud overhead. Apocalypse is nearing. Look at the crowd shot that has the Orthodox Jews in the foreground. Find the guy with orange hair. See how he clearly mouths,

"Oh my god!" and then — for no discernable reason — jumps up and down clapping delightedly? Does that seem authentic or appropriate to you?

No role is too small to be honest and specific. Even if you are simply one of many nameless thugs sitting in a hideout before Batman crashes through the window, you should be playing specific actions with specific goals, such as "I'm going to the fridge to get a beer for my friend Jimmy." "I am telling them about my favorite play from last night's football game." Believe it or not, the fact that you're doing something real will come across on camera, and it will be much better than intention-less sitting around.

Unless the director tells you to, **never look at the camera**, especially if you are background actor. You will instantly break the fourth wall, destroying the illusion of the show. When you're in a big crowd shot, before action is called, try to get a rough idea of where the camera is going to be so you don't look into the lens by mistake. I often have crowd shots where fifty people are acting perfectly, but one actor ruins it by looking into the camera. Fifty people, now consigned to the cutting room floor, because of one person. Don't be that person!

Sometimes I can't use the lead actor's best take because a background actor is doing something strange. For example, I had a scene where a Squad Leader was briefing his team on how they're going to search a building. The Squad Leader was pointing to the map, saying, "Red Team will go here, Blue Team is gonna take this corridor, then we rendezvous here." The background actor playing the Blue Team Leader stood right next to the Squad Leader. He nodded and nodded as the Squad Leader pointed out where everyone was to go — but he never once looked at the map that was being pointed to. By ignoring the map, he's defeating the whole point of the scene. How can I use any shot that clearly shows this error? I can't.

So the wide shot never made it into the scene. Instead, I used a close shot of the Squad Leader so the audience wouldn't know that the soldier next to him was doing the wrong thing. The director was not pleased when he saw this in the cutting room, but once he saw what the Blue Team Leader was doing, he understood. As is often the case, on set the director was focusing on the most important performance in the scene (the Squad Leader's) and also worrying about all the other material that needed to be filmed that day. He had so much going on that he didn't notice that the Blue Team Leader was ruining his shot. After they see something like that in the cutting room, some directors will contact the assistant directors and tell them to avoid hiring those background players again.

CHAPTER 10

HOW TO BEHAVE
AFTER YOUR BIG DAY

Success is not a destination, but the road that you're on.
You can only live your dream by working hard towards it.

— *Marlon Wayans*

You've shot your scene(s), and you want a copy of the work to put on your reel ASAP so you can use it to get more bookings. A very natural impulse. But take my advice — don't call the show and ask for dailies or cuts in progress. That's a big no-no. All of the networks and movie studios are very concerned with piracy and leaks, so they are definitely not going to send you a clip from an episode that hasn't aired or a movie that isn't in the theaters yet. It's especially true if you were in a hit drama or franchise film, where everyone is very concerned about plot details leaking onto the Internet.

Don't bother contacting the Editorial department to ask for dailies or the completed scene(s), because they will say no. Anybody who gave them to you could be fired.

After the show has aired or the movie has been released, is it OK to call the network or production office for a copy? Again, the answer is no. It's not standard practice to give actors that material, and nobody wants to put themselves at risk by making an exception for you. For TV shows, you can get a copy from iTunes very soon after the air date. If you're willing to wait a few months, you can buy the season DVDs or Blu-rays when they come out. A resourceful editor will know how to get material from these sources onto your reel.

If you find out that your scene was deleted, don't call the Editorial department — or anyone else — to ask why. We can't discuss the creative choices that were made. It would violate our creative collaboration with our producers and directors, and they won't re-hire any editor or other crew member who breaks that confidentiality. So don't ask, because it puts us in an terribly awkward position, and in the end, you won't get an answer. I understand this can be very frustrating. You've put yourself out there, and you want to know why your work was cut out. I wish our business operated differently, and there was a system whereby actors could get honest feedback about the choices that were made for their particular situation. But unfortunately, that's not how it works.

If your scene was cut out, keep your fingers crossed that it was good enough to be included in the "Deleted Scenes" on the season DVDs. Not every deleted scene makes it. Just the ones that are interesting enough to watch as stand-alone scenes. If your scene isn't on the DVDs, then you should probably infer that the scene was boring or turned out poorly, and be thankful nobody is ever going to see it.

CHAPTER 11

THAT'S A WRAP!

Knowledge isn't power until it is applied.

— *Dale Carnegie*

Remember:

There are a lot of things you can control... and a few things you can't.

Take this opportunity to focus on what you can control, because there's no point in focusing on what you can't. If you don't make the final cut, I hope you'll remember that if your technical performance was up to snuff and your acting was good, you probably were cut out for story reasons. And there was nothing you could have done about it, so forgive yourself and move on.

Keep in mind that actors are very beloved by writers, producers, directors and editors. We want to showcase you, because you make the words and story come alive. We think you're great! I hope that with the help of the information in this book, you'll have a long and fulfilling career — one that is on screen, far away from the cutting room floor.

Yours,
Jordan Goldman, A.C.E.

If you enjoyed this book, please consider leaving a positive review online where you purchased it. Your personal recommendation is the highest praise I can receive.

You can sign up for my email list online at EditorsAdviceForActors.com. I'll keep you up-to-date on future editions and live appearances. I will never share or sell your personal information.

I tweet as @theJGoldman.

You can like the book's Facebook page at: www.facebook.com/HowToAvoidTheCuttingRoomFloor.

My IMDb entry is located at: www.imdb.com/name/nm0325813/

THANKS & ACKNOWLEDGMENTS

To my wonderful partner in life, my amazing wife Katie Grant. She's creative, supportive, and brilliant. Katie was the one who, after listening to me gripe about an acting problem I'd had to fix at work that day, said "Actors don't know this stuff, Jordan!" and therefore inspired this book.

The many showrunners and directors I've been privileged to work with and learn from. Especially Shawn Ryan and Scott Brazil of *The Shield*, who gave me the big break that changed my life, and then took the time to teach me how to be a good editor on one of the greatest shows I could ever have been lucky enough to work on.

The actors I've had the joy to watch and edit. From the big stars like Michael Chiklis, Damian Lewis, and Claire Danes to the one-line day players, thank you for letting me into your craft and giving me such rich material to work with. Nobody knows your work better than the editor, and there's nobody in a position to admire it more than us.

My family, for supporting my dream of working in this crazy industry.

Hisham Abed, who took all of the photos and gave me wonderful advice about self-publishing. A great cinematographer and photographer, and a supreme collaborator. Check out more of his great work at hishamabed.com

My actors Gillian Shure, Colin Walker (thecolinwalker.com), and Heather Adair. Thank you for bringing *Blackmailed Beauty* to life, and being willing to be permanently immortalized demonstrating what NOT to do.

Michael Chiklis and Stephen Kay, for their encouragement and critical eyes.

Dallas Travers, who let me test out this material on her Thriving Artist Circle members. Actors should check out this valuable resource at thrivingartistcircle.com

Marsela, Jo, and Karen at KJ's Diner & Restaurant, where we photographed *Blackmailed Beauty*.

David Wienir, Steve Cohen A.C.E., Andy Saks, Norman Hollyn, Rich Bleiweiss, my readers/proofers, and everyone else who encouraged this project along the way!

Made in the USA
Lexington, KY
18 July 2018